Solar System Explorers

Earth

Written by
Charis Mather

KidHaven
PUBLISHING

Published in 2026 by
KidHaven Publishing, an Imprint of
Greenhaven Publishing, LLC
2544 Clinton St., Buffalo, NY 14224

Written by: Charis Mather
Edited by: Noah Leatherland
Designed by: Rob Delph

Cataloging-in-Publication Data
Names: Mather, Charis.
Title: Earth / Charis Mather.
Description: Buffalo, NY : Kidhaven Publishing, 2026. | Series: Solar System Explorers | Includes glossary and index
Identifiers: ISBN 9781534549739 (pbk) | ISBN 9781534549746 (library bound) | ISBN 9781534549753 (ebook)
Subjects: LCSH: Earth (Planet)—Juvenile Literature
Classification: LCC QB637.4 M38 2026 | DDC 525 --dc25

Manufactured in the United States of America

CPSIA compliance information: Batch #CSKH26
For further information contact Greenhaven Publishing LLC
at 1-844-317-7404.

Please visit our website,
www.greenhavenpublishing.com.
For a free color catalog of all our high-quality books, call toll free 1-844-317-7404
or fax 1-844-317-7405.

Find us on

Image Credits

Images are courtesy of Shutterstock.com. With thanks to Getty Images, Thinkstock Photo and iStockphoto. Cover – 19 STUDIO, aappp, AspctStyle, andreysharonov, leshiy985. Recurring Images – aappp, thomas eder, YummyBuum, Sabelskaya. 4–5 – 24K-Production, WinWin artlab. 6–7 – alexaldo, Vadim Sadovski. 8–9 – Stanimir G.Stoev, Dr_Flash. 12–13 – worldswildlifewonders, Vadim Sadovski. 14–15 – Earth Science and Remote Sensing Unit, Lyndon B. Johnson Space Center, Public domain, via Wikimedia Commons, Calin Tatu. 16–17 – Anest, Valentin Ayupov. 18–19 – JLStock, Dima Zel. 20–21 – Kelly Headrick, shutter_tonko. 22–23 – 24K-Production, Alones.

Contents

Words that look like this can be found in the glossary on page 24.

Let's Explore!

Have you ever looked up at space and wondered what is out there? We have! As solar system explorers, our mission is to find out everything we can about the planets around the sun.

Exploring the solar system is a big job. The solar system includes the sun, eight planets, five dwarf planets, and hundreds of moons. Everything in the solar system **orbits** the sun.

Where Is Earth?

All the planets are constantly orbiting the sun along their own paths. If they were all lined up in order, this is how they would look:

Earth is the third of the solar system's eight planets.

Earth is about 93 million miles (150 million km) away from the sun. That might sound far, but the solar system is so enormous that it is a short distance compared to some other planets.

Round and Round

It takes about 365 days for Earth to orbit the sun once. That is one year.

Different parts of Earth get different amounts of sunlight through the year. This causes **seasons**.

Earth spins as it orbits the sun. It takes 24 hours for Earth to complete one spin. That is one day.

Daytime and nighttime are caused by Earth spinning into and out of the sun's light.

Planet Profile

Here is what we know about Earth so far.

Temperature

Water freezes at 32 degrees Fahrenheit (0°C)

Earth's average surface temperature is 59°F (15°C).

Size

- Around: About 25,000 miles (40,000 km)
- Across: About 7,900 miles (12,700 km)

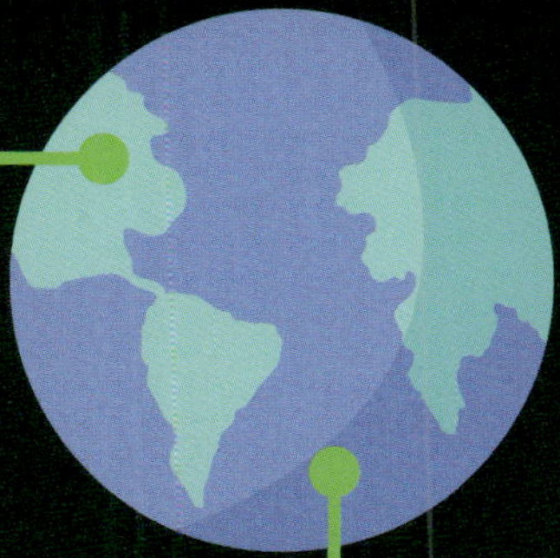

Water boils at 212°F (100°C).

What Is Earth Made Of?

The main materials that make up Earth are oxygen, silicon, aluminum, and iron.

Earth is a rocky, or terrestrial, planet. That means it has a hard surface and is mainly made of rocks and metals. Most of Earth's surface is covered in water.

Earth has four main layers.

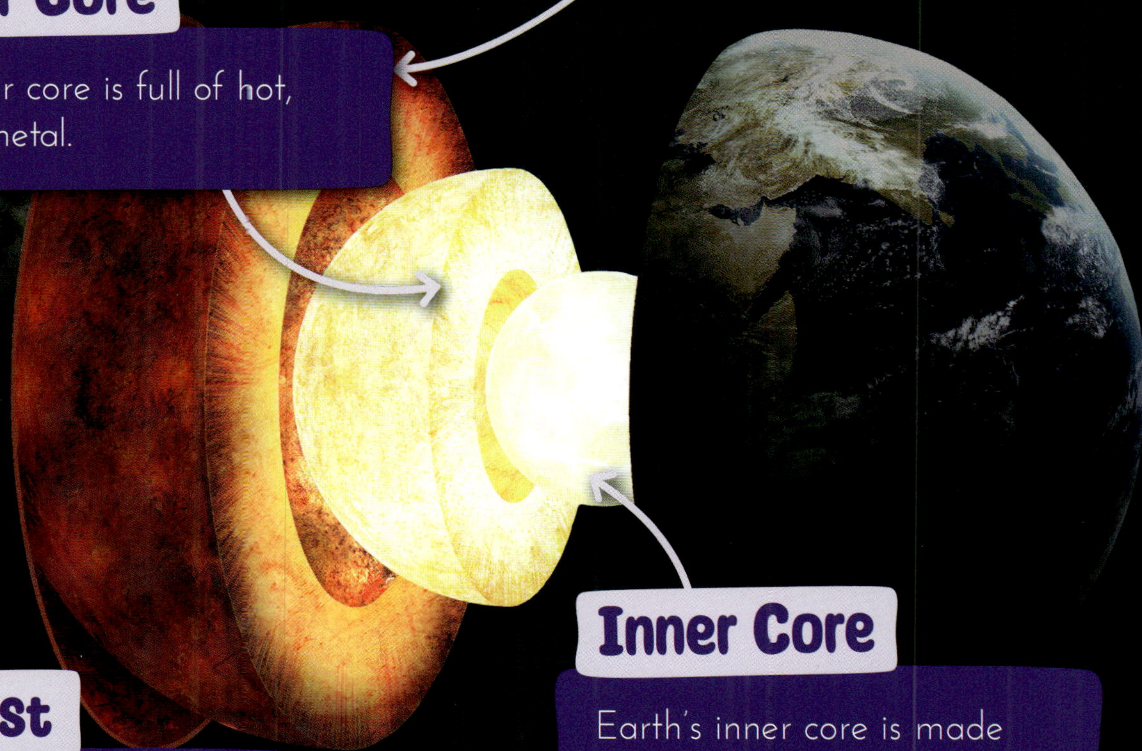

Mantle

The mantle layer is made of hot, rocky material.

Outer Core

The outer core is full of hot, melted metal.

Inner Core

Earth's inner core is made of extremely hot metal.

Crust

Earth's outer layer is made up of rocks, metals, and water.

Watching the Weather

Around Earth, there is a layer of air called the atmosphere. The atmosphere is made up of lots of different types of **gases**. Earth's atmosphere contains nitrogen, oxygen, and carbon dioxide.

The gases in Earth's atmosphere help make the sky look blue.

The atmosphere is important for many reasons.

It traps in the sun's heat.

It keeps in water and allows clouds to form.

It causes wind and different kinds of weather.

It protects Earth from **meteors**.

Is There Life On Earth?

Earth is the only planet in the entire solar system where life has been found. Plants, mushrooms, and animals are all different kinds of life that call Earth home.

Humans are a kind of life too.

Earth has the perfect **conditions** for life. Its atmosphere and distance from the sun make it the perfect temperature. There is plenty of water, which all living things need.

Spot the Satellites

Anything in space that orbits a bigger object is called a satellite. Satellites can be **natural** or human-made.

The moon is Earth's only natural satellite. It takes around 27 days for the moon to orbit Earth.

Humans have sent thousands of satellites into Earth's orbit. The International Space Station is a human-made satellite that people use to learn about Earth and space. It orbits Earth every 90 minutes.

Scientists from many countries have lived on the International Space Station.

Terrific Tides

Earth's natural satellite, the moon, has a small amount of **gravity**. While the moon's gravity is much weaker than Earth's, it is still strong enough to pull at Earth's water. This causes tides.

Tides are large ocean waves that affect the water level. The parts of the planet that are closest to the moon and farthest from the moon have the highest water levels.

More to Explore

We have learned so many fascinating facts about Earth on this mission. It is time to wave goodbye to this beautiful blue planet and blast off to another.

There are so many o-her places to explore in this spectacular solar system. There is so much more to find out!

Glossary

conditions the state of the environment, such as the temperature, rainfall and food available

degrees a measuring unit used to explain how hot or cold something is

gases things that are like air, which fill any space available

gravity the force that pulls everything downward toward the center of large objects in space

meteors chunks of rock or metal from space that pass through and burn up in Earth's atmosphere

natural found in nature and not made by people

orbits moves around a star or planet in a curved path

seasons different parts of the year based on changes in the planet's position around the sun

surface the top or outer layer of something

Index